SUPERHEROES OF SCIENCE

SIR ISAAC NEWTON

OVERLORD OF GRAVITY

Angela Royston

Gareth Stevens
PUBLISHING

Please visit our website, **www.garethstevens.com**. For a free color catalog of all our high-quality books, call toll free 1-800-542-2595 or fax 1-877-542-2596.

Library of Congress Cataloging-in-Publication Data

Royston, Angela.

Sir Isaac Newton: overlord of gravity / by Angela Royston.

p. cm. – (Superheroes of science)

Includes index.

ISBN 978-1-4824-3153-7 (pbk.)

ISBN 978-1-4824-3156-8 (6 pack)

ISBN 978-1-4824-3154-4 (library binding)

1. Newton, Isaac, – 1642-1727 – Juvenile literature. 2. Scientists – England – Biography – Juvenile literature. I. Royston, Angela. II. Title.

QC16.N7 D53 2016

530–d23

First Edition

Published in 2016 by

Gareth Stevens Publishing

111 East 14th Street, Suite 349

New York, NY 10003

© 2016 Gareth Stevens Publishing

Produced for Gareth Stevens by Calcium

Editors for Calcium: 3REDCARS

Designers: Paul Myerscough and 3REDCARS

Picture credits: Cover art by Mat Edwards; Dreamstime: Anizza 45b, Anthony Baggett 9t, 19t, Dannyphoto80 5b, Effectteam 31b, Michael Foley 7t, Kari Høglund 30c, Jerryway 20c, Johnhill118 11t, Georgios Kollidas 4c, 8b, 27c, 35c, 43t, Vitaly Korovin 25b, KTS 21b, Olivier Le Queinec 26c, Subhrajyoti Parida 42c, 2ndpic 22c, Tonito84 15t; Shutterstock: Aspen Photo 15c, Bobboz 33t, Maksim Budnikov 32c, David Burrows 41t, Georgios Kollidas 44c, David Koscheck 16t, Pshenichka 24c; Wellcome Library, London: 35t, 23b, 36c, 39b; Wikimedia Commons: 29b, 40c, David Brewster 18b, National Aeronautics and Space Administration (NASA) 12c, Royal Society 17c.

Printed in the United States of America

CPSIA compliance information: Batch #CS15GS: For further information contact Gareth Stevens, New York, New York at 1-800-542-2595.

CONTENTS

Chapter 1
AN EXTRAORDINARY MIND

Isaac Newton lived around 300 years ago, when it was fashionable for men to wear long, curly wigs. Even eminent scientists wanted to look their best!

Kpow!

Isaac Newton did not grow up expecting to become a superhero scientist. He had a lonely childhood, without his parents and with few friends. He continued to spend most of his life on his own, but he put his time to excellent use. His favorite activities were unusual–thinking and mathematics.

From an early age, things that most people take for granted intrigued him. We know that objects drop to the ground, and that something will move if you push it hard enough. What made Newton extraordinary was that he looked at everyday things, such as light and forces, and used mathematics to unravel their mysteries.

Newton lived during a time called "The Enlightenment," when scholars in Western Europe began to question traditional truths and to use reason to think for themselves. Newton worked very much as a modern scientist does today. He used mathematics, experiments, and scientific method to test his ideas. As a result, he changed the way people understand the world and even beyond.

Scientific Curiosity

Newton asked himself fascinating questions about the world and the universe. He wondered, for instance, how something that is constantly changing could be measured, what force keeps an object in space orbiting another, or what produces the colors in a rainbow. He had the energy and intellect to probe and analyze such puzzling problems, coming up with brilliant, mathematically based theories that made him the leading scientist of his day.

STAR CONTRIBUTION

Newton was the first person to figure out how and why an object in space circles, or orbits, another object. He came up with a "thought experiment" to show how an imaginary cannon, set higher than the highest mountain, could send a cannonball into orbit around Earth. On October 4, 1957, more than 250 years later, Russian scientists launched *Sputnik 1*, the first manmade satellite, into space. They could not have done it without Newton's discoveries.

Newton's incredible achievements are even more extraordinary because he made them without the help of calculators or computers. Today, astrophysicists use computers to figure out the orbits of the planets and their moons. Newton did his calculations using just mathematics and observations.

Sputnik 1 was the first artificial satellite to orbit Earth and so the first to make Newton's "thought experiment" a reality.

TROUBLES AND TRIUMPHS

Isaac Newton was not a particularly smart child and was expected to become a farmer, like his father. However, he managed to develop his amazing abilities through a combination of misfortune, good luck, and determination.

The misfortune began early. Three months before Newton was born, on Christmas Day, December 25, 1642, his father died. Newton's bad luck continued when his mother, Hannah, remarried when he was three years old and left him with his grandmother in Woolsthorpe, a village in Lincolnshire, England. Newton was very unhappy and often angry. He hated his stepfather and once threatened to burn down his house. Although his stepfather died in 1653, Newton's life did not improve when Hannah returned to Woolsthorpe, bringing with her three young children.

Although Newton's father had been a wealthy and successful farmer, he was unable to read and write. Isaac, however, attended classes in village schools near Woolsthorpe. His luck changed for the better in 1654 when he was sent to King's School in Grantham, a town about 7 miles (11 km) away. It was too far from Woolsthorpe for a daily journey, so Newton stayed with the family of an apothecary—someone who prepared and sold medicines. The apothecary had three stepchildren —two sons and a daughter. Isaac hated the sons but was friends with Catherine, the daughter.

Testing Time

From a very young age, Newton wanted to experiment and understand natural forces, such as motion and time. When he was just nine years old, he carved his own sundial in stone. Sundials have a plate marked out like a clock and a pointer that casts shadows on the plate during daylight. As the sun's position changes, the shadows differ in length and position, indicating what time it is.

SUPERHERO FACT

Newton spent his early days at Woolsthorpe Manor. It is now a museum dedicated to the scientist.

Although he made no friends at school and did not impress his teachers, Newton continued to be curious about the world. He borrowed books from the church library and spent much of his time making models, such as windmills and sundials, and inventing things. Eventually, the headmaster realized that Newton had special talents.

When Newton was 17, though, bad luck struck again—his mother took him out of school to work on the family farm. Fortunately, he was so bad at running the farm that his uncle, William Ayscough, sent him back to school. Both Ayscough and Newton's headmaster agreed that the best future for the boy was to go to the University of Cambridge. This was Newton's chance to escape!

INDEPENDENT THINKER

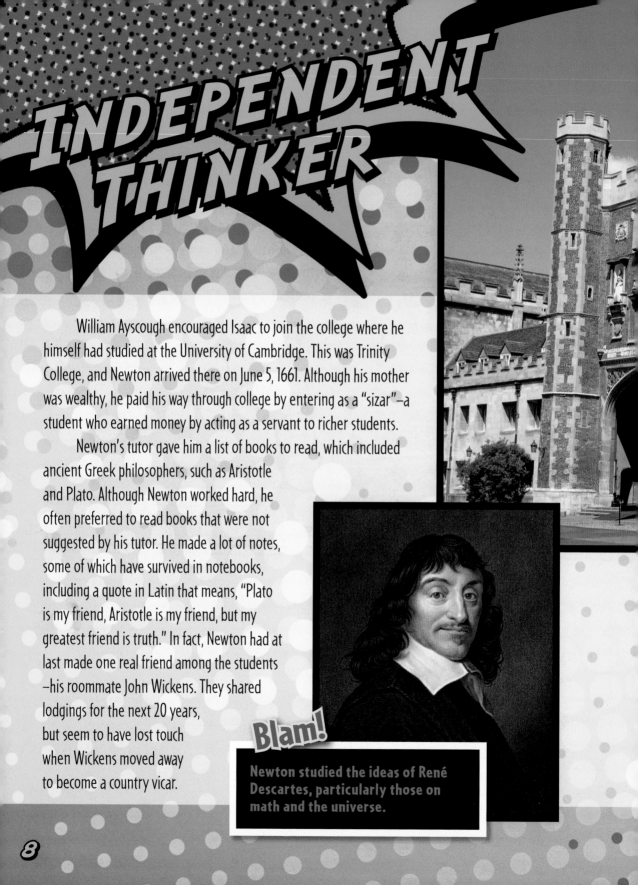

William Ayscough encouraged Isaac to join the college where he himself had studied at the University of Cambridge. This was Trinity College, and Newton arrived there on June 5, 1661. Although his mother was wealthy, he paid his way through college by entering as a "sizar"–a student who earned money by acting as a servant to richer students.

Newton's tutor gave him a list of books to read, which included ancient Greek philosophers, such as Aristotle and Plato. Although Newton worked hard, he often preferred to read books that were not suggested by his tutor. He made a lot of notes, some of which have survived in notebooks, including a quote in Latin that means, "Plato is my friend, Aristotle is my friend, but my greatest friend is truth." In fact, Newton had at last made one real friend among the students –his roommate John Wickens. They shared lodgings for the next 20 years, but seem to have lost touch when Wickens moved away to become a country vicar.

Blam!

Newton studied the ideas of René Descartes, particularly those on math and the universe.

Smart Solutions

Newton's study of Descartes and an English mathematician named John Wallis influenced his thoughts about measuring something that is constantly changing. For example, how could the area under a curve be measured when it is different at every point of the curve? Newton—and later Gottfried Leibniz, a German mathematician and philosopher—independently hit on the same solution. Newton named the new mathematics "fluxions," but it is now known as calculus.

Trinity College, where Newton studied, is one of many colleges at the University of Cambridge. The college buildings are unchanged.

Newton did not shine at his studies, nor did he impress his university teachers. In 1664, his mathematics professor, Isaac Barrow, tested him on the ideas on geometry proposed by the ancient Greek mathematician Euclid. He thought that Newton's response was very poor, but Newton was actually way ahead of Barrow. Newton had been studying the recent ideas of René Descartes, a French mathematician and philosopher, which were unknown to Barrow and went far beyond those of Euclid. In 1665, Newton completed his bachelor's degree, but he was not awarded a distinction or honors.

THE PLAGUE YEARS

During 1665 and 1666, bubonic plague swept through London and other parts of England. This terrible disease spread rapidly and killed thousands of people. The best way to combat the plague was to keep people away from each other, and so, in the summer of 1665, the University of Cambridge closed, and the students were sent home. For Newton, who had just completed his bachelor's degree, this was a stroke of good luck because it gave him freedom and time to develop his ideas.

Newton returned to Woolsthorpe in August 1665. He took his textbooks and notebooks with him, and he continued to work and think. There is

SUPERHERO FACT

Rapid Progress

Newton's extraordinary research during the plague years—on topics including calculus, light, gravity, the movement of planets, and natural laws of motion—transformed his academic career. When he returned to Trinity College in 1667, he was made a minor fellow (a member of the college staff). Before his 27th birthday, in 1669, he became Lucasian Professor of Mathematics, succeeding Isaac Barrow, the professor who had given him a bad grade!

In September 1665, the plague reached Eyam in Derbyshire. The villagers isolated themselves so that infection did not spread to other places, like Woolsthorpe.

PLAGUE COTTAGE

Mary Hadfield, formerly Cooper, lived here with her two sons, Edward and Jonathan, her new husband, Alexander Hadfield and an employed hand George Viccars

George Viccars, the first plague victim, died on 7th September 1665

a world-famous story–which may or may not be true–that Newton was sitting under an apple tree at Woolsthorpe, when an apple fell to the ground. It is said that this set him thinking about gravity, and how its force keeps the moon in motion around the sun.

Gravity was not the only issue that Newton studied. He carried out experiments and looked for answers to other difficult questions, such as how to measure things that are constantly moving, and the nature of color and light. When he later recalled the two plague years of 1665 and 1666, Newton said, "In those days I was in my prime of age for invention, and minded mathematics and philosophy more than at any time since."

In September 1666, a great fire broke out in London, which destroyed many buildings but helped to clear the city of plague. This was followed by an easing of plague deaths elsewhere in England, and by March 1667 it was safe for Newton to return to Cambridge and pursue further studies.

Chapter 2

NEWTON'S LAWS OF MOTION

At Woolsthorpe, during the plague years, Newton was working on his ideas about forces and motion. However, he did not publish his theories until 1687–in *Philosophiae Naturalis Principia Mathematica* ("Mathematical Principles of Natural Philosophy"). This book was to become one of the most famous and influential ever written. It included Newton's three laws of motion, which described and explained the movement of objects in every situation–from the particles inside atoms to the galaxies of stars. The laws were unchallenged for more than 200 years, until Albert Einstein developed his theory of relativity.

The first law of motion is also named the law of inertia. Inertia is a state in which something, or someone, resists change. Newton's law states that a stationary object will remain at rest unless it is pushed or pulled by a force. Similarly, an object moving in a straight line at a steady speed will continue to do so, unless a force pushes or pulls it.

Although the laws of motion are named after Newton, René Descartes actually discovered the first law in the year that Newton

Zoom!

Newton's first law of motion shows that *Voyager 1*, which was launched on August 4, 1977, could now go on traveling through space forever.

No Stopping It

A modern example of Newton's law of inertia is the spacecraft *Voyager I*, which was launched in 1977 and is now traveling—without power—at 38,000 miles per hour (61,200 kph) in a straight line through space. There are no forces to slow it down or change its direction. It has already left the solar system, and it will keep moving at the same rate and in the same direction, unless an external force stops it.

SUPERHERO STAT

was born. Newton did not steal Descartes's idea—he developed it. The second law, which defines force in terms of mass and acceleration, and the third law, which shows how each object reacts to the force of another, are Newton's own work. Newton later said, "If I have seen further, it is by standing on the shoulders of giants," meaning that his work is built on the work of earlier thinkers. The comment, however, may also have been an insult to his fellow scientist Robert Hooke, because Hooke was unusually small in height!

Crash!

If a car suddenly stops, the driver and passengers still move forward. Seat belts were invented to protect you from the dangers of inertia!

FOLLOW THE FORCE

Newton's second law deals with the effect of a force on an object. It says that when a force acts on an object, the object will change velocity. Velocity is the scientific name for movement–the speed at which something moves in a specific direction, such as a truck heading south at 50 miles per hour (80 kph).

A force is needed to make an object move or change speed, or direction. The bigger the force, the bigger the change. For example, when you kick a ball, your foot applies the force, and the ball moves in the direction of your foot. The harder you kick it, the faster it will move. However, what happens when you kick a heavier ball? If you apply the same force, it will travel more slowly, while a lighter ball will travel faster.

If someone intercepts the ball, its speed and direction will change. A moving object can also transfer force to another object. In a game of pool, for example, a

SUPERHERO STAT

Newton's Very Own Force

Newton's work on forces was so groundbreaking that his name has been given to a unit of force. One Newton is the force required to make an object weighing 2.2 pounds (1 kg) accelerate at 3.3 feet (1 m) per second squared.

In pool, players use a long stick, or cue, to hit one ball with another. The skill is applying the right amount of force in the right direction.

player might apply a force to one ball so that it hits another ball, which will affect the speed and direction of both balls.

For Newton, it was not enough to know that hitting, pushing, or kicking an object makes it move. He wanted to know how and why, and figured out the relationship between force, mass (or weight), and acceleration—the rate of change of speed. He expressed the result in his now-famous equation $F = ma$, where "F" is the size of the force, "m" is the mass of the object, and "a" is the acceleration.

Mass is a measure of the amount of matter an object contains— on Earth, an object's mass is equivalent to its weight.

Pow!

The harder the football player kicks the ball, the faster it accelerates. The shape of the ball makes it difficult to control the direction the ball takes after it bounces.

ACTION AND REACTION

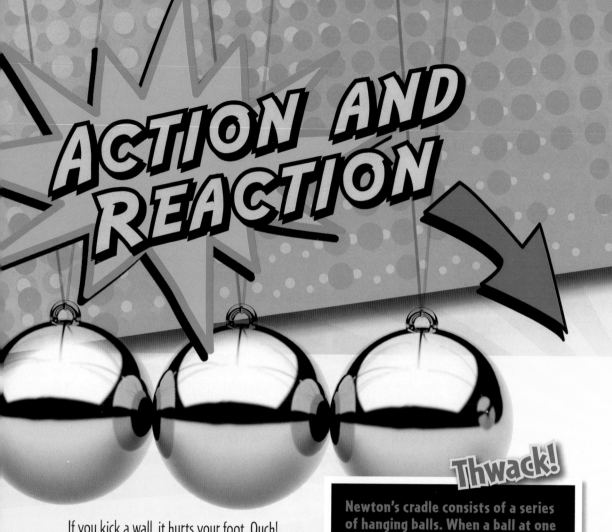

Thwack!

Newton's cradle consists of a series of hanging balls. When a ball at one end is pulled out, it falls back, but only the other end ball swings out. The energy created by the first ball passes through the middle balls and out through the end ball.

If you kick a wall, it hurts your foot. Ouch! That is because the wall reacts to the force of your kick. This illustrates Newton's third law of motion, which says that when a force acts on an object, the object reacts with an equal but opposite force.

For example, when you sit on a chair, your weight pushes down on the chair, but the chair pushes up with an equal force. You may not feel the force of the chair pushing up, but think what would happen if the chair did not resist. If your weight were greater than the chair's ability to push back, the chair would collapse. However, if the chair pushed back with greater force, you would bounce up into the air!

Precious Notebooks

Throughout his life, Newton recorded his thoughts, calculations, and experiments in a series of notebooks. The surviving notebooks are preserved at Cambridge University Library. One, entitled *The Lawes of Motion*, contains work from the years 1665 to 1672. Other notebooks cover religion, philosophy, and alchemy, as well as mathematics and science. They show how wide ranging, yet detailed, Newton's thoughts were—and remain an important legacy for historians and scientists today.

SUPERHERO FACT

Newton took great care to write down all his ideas and theories. He even used the margins of his notebooks to do the math.

Similarly, in a swimming pool, you can push against the side of the pool to push yourself off. What actually happens is that when you push the side of the pool, it reacts by pushing back with an equal force, although you cannot feel it pushing you away. However, compare what happens if you push against a floating ball in the pool. When you push the lighter ball, it moves away from you. Because you are heavier, or in scientific terms, you have a larger mass, the ball does not push you backward. Your weight means that you exert the greater force, as Newton's second law explains.

Newton's laws of motion explained many other things, such as momentum—the combination of mass and velocity that gives things the energy to move. In Newton's cradle, the momentum of the swinging ball passes from one ball to the next until it reaches the final ball, which then moves.

Chapter 3

RISING STAR OF SCIENCE

When Newton returned to the University of Cambridge in April 1667, there was one obstacle in the way of him continuing his work at Trinity College. He needed to be elected a minor fellow —a post that would be the first step toward a teaching career at the university. Luckily, Newton was elected and in the next two years he raced ahead. He gained a master's degree in 1668 and was then promoted to become a senior fellow, a more important teaching post.

Newton's biggest breakthrough came in 1669, when he was appointed to succeed his former mathematics professor, Isaac Barrow. Barrow had once thought that Newton had a poor knowledge of geometry, but he had since become one of his greatest admirers. Yet, it seems that Newton was such an uninspiring teacher that few students came to his lectures.

Newton's reflecting telescope was smaller than previous telescopes. Its two tubes could be slid together to focus the image.

Improved Vision

In his laboratory shed, Newton created the first-ever reflecting telescope, which he used to study the planets. Telescopes at that time used glass lenses to enlarge the view of a star or planet, but these produced a blurred image. By using mirrors instead, Newton produced a much clearer image, magnified between 30 and 40 times. A shiny, curved mirror at the bottom of the telescope collected the light and reflected it onto a flat mirror, which in turn reflected it at a 90° angle, so that it could be seen through the eyepiece.

STAR CONTRIBUTION

This statue of Newton stands outside Trinity College, Cambridge. Most of Newton's scientific work was done while he was at Trinity.

In fact, this proved useful, as it gave him more time to pursue his own interests and studies.

During 1668 and 1669, Newton set up a mini-laboratory in a shed in the grounds of Trinity College. At this time, Newton was interested in the nature of light and color, and how the human eye interprets them. He carried out some dangerous optical experiments on himself, which should definitely not be repeated! In one experiment, he described how he stuck a bodkin (a large, blunt needle) into his eye socket between the eyeball and the bone, and pressed it against the eyeball. His aim was to discover if the pressure would affect the colors he saw. According to his notebook, "there appeared severall white darke & colored circles," which became clearer when he moved the bodkin and fainter if he held it still.

RAINBOW SCIENCE

Because of his work on light, Newton understood why other existing telescopes produced a blurred image. He had observed that a beam of light refracts, or bends, as it moves from one material, such as air, to another, such as glass. Other telescopes were made using curved glass lenses, rather than the mirror he introduced in his reflecting telescope. Newton saw that it was the refractory effect of the glass in those instruments that distorted and blurred the image.

You can see refraction if you put a teaspoon into a glass tumbler, half-filled with water. The spoon appears to bend and change direction as it enters the water. Scientists already knew that a rainbow was caused by light refracting when it passed through raindrops, but they could not understand where the colors came from. Some thought that the colors must come from the water. Scientists also knew that a glass prism—a clear, three-sided glass object—produced a spectrum of colors, but that, they said, came from the glass.

Newton set up an experiment to convince his colleagues that the colors were contained in

Wow!

The colors in a rainbow are produced when sunlight passes through raindrops. The refracted light forms an arc.

Light and Color

Before Newton's prism experiment, scientists thought that white light was a single, basic unit, which could not be divided. Newton showed that white light contains all the different colors of the spectrum. When white light passes through a prism, each color refracts at a slightly different angle to create a spectrum of different colors.

STAR CONTRIBUTION

the light itself. On a bright sunny day, he closed the shutters across the windows of his room, so that only a thin beam of light shone through. He placed a prism on a table, so that the light passed through the prism. As the light came out the other side, it was no longer a clear beam but a range of colors—the same as those in a rainbow. He then took a second prism and turned it upside down, so that the bright band of colors from the first prism passed through it. The result was a beam of white light, which was created by reuniting all the colors.

When light passes through a prism, it refracts or bends to form bands of colored light. Each color bends at a different angle.

SCIENCE WARS

Newton's work on his new reflecting telescope brought him to the attention of the Royal Society, a group of pioneering philosophers and mathematicians, based in London. In 1672, after showing the telescope to Society members, Newton was elected to be a Fellow of the Society—a significant honor. His work on the composition of light brought him even more acclaim.

Newton published his first scientific paper in the Society's journal, *Philosophical Transactions of the Royal Society*. The paper was on light and color, and in it Newton explained how white light contains the spectrum of colors. He also argued that his experiments showed that light consists of small particles, rather than waves of energy, as many scientists thought. This led to a serious disagreement between Newton and Robert Hooke, a leading scientist at the Royal Society.

Hooke said that Newton's conclusion about particles of light was not proven by his experiments. He maintained that light came in waves. Newton was furious about

Whoosh!

A beam of light can be made up of waves or particles, although they are invisible. Newton thought that light consisted of only particles.

Great Minds Think Alike

The Royal Society began in the 1640s, when a group of scientists met each week to discuss their work and share their experiments. Their aim was to show that knowledge about natural phenomena—the science of why natural events occur—came from observation and through experiments. The Society's motto is still *Nullius in verba*, which is Latin for "Take nobody's word for it." Although Newton largely withdrew from the Society during Hooke's life, he was elected its president in 1703 and remained so until his death in 1727.

Hooke's criticisms and rejected them. In fact, both men were correct. Today, scientists accept that light sometimes acts as a wave and sometimes as particles. In 1675, Newton published another paper on light. This time, Hooke claimed that Newton had stolen the results of some of his experiments. This was not true, but Newton remained in Cambridge and decided to keep away from Robert Hooke and the Royal Society.

Scientists often met at the Royal Society in London to discuss their ideas. Newton himself is the chairman at this meeting.

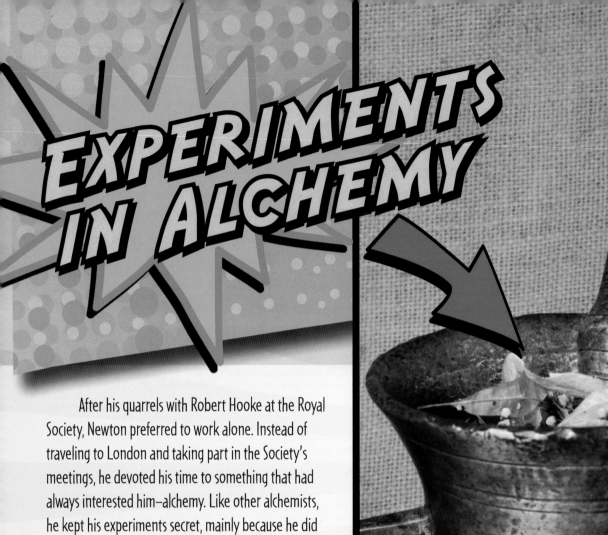

EXPERIMENTS IN ALCHEMY

After his quarrels with Robert Hooke at the Royal Society, Newton preferred to work alone. Instead of traveling to London and taking part in the Society's meetings, he devoted his time to something that had always interested him—alchemy. Like other alchemists, he kept his experiments secret, mainly because he did not want them to be stolen, but also because they were considered to be more magic than science.

Alchemy had been pursued for centuries in Egypt, the Far East, Arabia, and Europe. It was thought that gold was the perfect metal and that all other metals were impure. Alchemists searched for what they named the "philosopher's stone," which would change any metal into gold. Clearly, whoever found it would become very rich!

Apothecaries used a mortar and pestle to grind the ingredients of medicines. Alchemists used this and other tools in their experiments.

Particle Prophet

Although Newton's interest in alchemy might seem out of keeping with his rational approach to science, the two were not entirely separate. Both sprang from his curiosity about all natural things. In attempting to "purify" metals, Newton worked on the idea that materials and light were made up of tiny, indivisible particles. In that, he was ahead of his time. Today, scientists in the field of advanced physics, such as particle physics and quantum physics, name those particles atoms and photons.

STAR CONTRIBUTION

While the many experiments of alchemists did not succeed in changing metals into other metals, their work fed into an understanding of how certain metals react to produce other substances. Alchemy provided the foundation for chemistry.

Newton's interest in alchemy probably began when he was still at school in Grantham, lodging with the apothecary William Clark and his family. He would have seen Clark mixing potions from powders, herbs, and oils to make medicines. Watching the bubbling, fizzy flasks of liquid must have fascinated young Newton.

Newton's notebooks on alchemy contain other alchemists' work as well as his own. Newton wanted to copy and understand these experiments.

Wow!

These gleaming stones are nuggets of pure gold. Alchemists searched for ways of changing other, less valuable metals into gold.

Chapter 4
DISCUSSION AND DISPUTE

The Royal Society, where scientists first met to test and discuss their experiments, had a major influence on good scientific practice. Robert Boyle–often named the "father of chemistry"–was one of the Society's founders in 1660 and one of the first scientists to publish details of his own work. Publishing the results and conclusions of experiments became an essential part of what is now termed the "scientific method." Evidence has to be measured, and experiments have to be described in detail so that other scientists can repeat them and confirm the findings.

When someone comes up with a scientific theory or law, a single instance of something failing to obey that rule will instantly make the theory suspect. For example, the force of gravity pulls things toward the center of Earth. If a place were found where this were not so,

Modern scientific experiments follow the scientific method pioneered by Robert Boyle, Newton, and others at the Royal Society.

Newton's Heroes

Like all scientists, Newton built theories on the ideas of earlier scientists. They included Nicolaus Copernicus, a Polish astronomer who first determined that Earth traveled around the sun, not the other way around as had been believed. Another was the Italian scientist Galileo, who studied inertia and the effect of gravity on falling objects, and was the first to use a telescope to study stars and planets. Johannes Kepler, a German astronomer who described how planets move around the sun, also influenced Newton's work.

SUPERHERO FACT

scientists would have to figure out why, or change their ideas about gravity!

Some scientists, including Newton, could not accept criticism easily. Robert Hooke was brusque and quick to criticize Newton, and this led to many quarrels between them. Newton was torn between wanting to publish his experiments and wanting to avoid criticism. For this reason, he often kept his work to himself and only published it when he was forced into doing so—perhaps because another scientist was about to publish the same idea. For example, he only published his work on calculus when Gottfried Leibniz began to publish papers on the same subject 20 years after Newton's own work.

Robert Boyle moved chemistry from the dubious world of alchemy into the regular world of science. Boyle had a big influence on Newton.

COMETS AND COFFEE

One subject that excited members of the Royal Society was astronomy. They were particularly interested in the movement of planets and comets. A comet is a type of large snowball made of ice, dust, and small pieces of rock. It sometimes orbits close to the sun but then swings far beyond the planets. Newton had seen his first comet in the winter of 1664-65. The amazing sight–with the comet's long tail trailing light across the night sky–fascinated him and Newton had made detailed notes about it. Later, at the Royal Society, he discussed astronomy with other scientists.

Newton was still wary of Robert Hooke and never liked him, but, by about the early 1680s, the two sometimes wrote to each other about subjects of mutual interest, including astronomy. Hooke, together with the astronomer Edmond Halley, and Christopher Wren (the acclaimed English architect of St. Paul's Cathedral in London, whose first love was science and mathematics) used to meet in the city's coffeehouses. In the seventeenth century, these were public social

Whoosh!

Halley's comet is an awesome sight in the night sky. Comets were once thought to be omens of disaster.

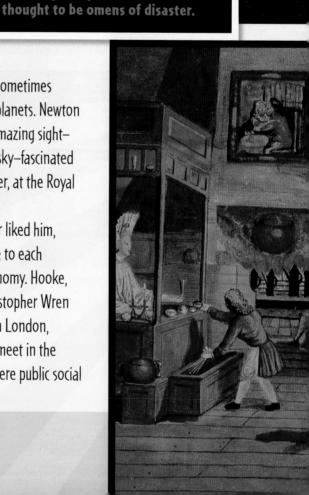

Comet Calculations

Newton's notebook from 1664 and 1665 includes details of the position of the comet compared to the position of nearby stars. Using these observations he was able to calculate the curved path of the comet. Newton's calculations allowed Edmond Halley to predict that a comet he observed in 1682 would return 76 or 77 years later, in 1758 or 1759. When his prediction proved to be accurate, the comet became known as Halley's Comet. This comet was last seen in 1986 and is predicted to next appear in 2061.

SUPERHERO FACT

places where people gathered to talk about business or the latest news.

The Society members would discuss topics such as gravity and the movement of planets. What especially intrigued the group was why comets appear and disappear, and they tried to predict when the next one would be seen. As Newton shared their passion for astronomy and was especially interested in comets, he is thought to have joined them whenever he came up to London from Cambridge.

Royal Society scientists often met up in coffeehouses. These popular meeting places first opened in London in the seventeenth century.

THE SECRETS OF GRAVITY

Gravity is a force of attraction between two objects. Like magnetism—the attraction between certain metals—gravity acts from a distance, as well as between objects in contact with each other. Unlike magnetism, gravity is at work between all objects, whatever material they are made of.

Newton had been thinking about gravity since 1665, when he was forced to return to Woolsthorpe at the time of plague. He wondered what force held the moon in orbit around Earth. His genius was to recognize that the moon was held by the same force of gravity that pulled falling objects toward the center of Earth.

Over the following 20 years, Newton developed his ideas about gravity and figured out his law of universal gravitation. With Robert Hooke, Edmond Halley, and Christopher Wren, he discussed the possible paths that the planets and comets took in orbiting the sun.

Newton realized that any two objects produce a force of attraction that works equally in both directions. A falling apple

A feather falls slowly through the air. Newton's formula proves that, without air resistance to slow them, all objects fall at the same speed.

Calculating Gravity

Newton's law of universal gravitation is given as an equation from which you can calculate the actual value of the force of gravity for any two objects at a particular distance. It is usually expressed as $F = G\frac{m_1 m_2}{r_2}$, where "F" is the force of attraction between the objects, "G" is a constant that is the same for all objects, whatever their mass, "m1" and "m2" are the masses of the two objects, and "r" is the distance between the centers of the objects. Newton's equation allowed astronomers to figure out the mass of planets and their distance from the sun from observations about their orbits.

STAR CONTRIBUTION

attracts the ground with the same force that pulls it down. He figured out that the strength of gravity depends on the mass of the objects and the distance between them, so the greater the mass of the objects, the greater the force of gravity. Newton also discovered that the force decreased as the distance between the objects increased. His work on gravity paved the way for the exploration of space. In 2014, the European Space Agency (ESA) used his laws to land Rosetta, an unmanned spacecraft, on a fast-moving comet.

The moon is much smaller and less dense than Earth. This means that gravity there is much weaker—only about one-sixth of that on Earth.

Chapter 5
PLANETS AND MOTION

We know that Earth is one of eight planets that orbit the sun. Mercury, Venus, Earth, and Mars are the rocky inner planets, while Jupiter (the biggest planet), Saturn, Uranus, and Neptune are vast balls of gas that form the outer planets. Planets and stars had fascinated astronomers since ancient times. However, when Newton was born, in 1642, relatively little was known about them.

The Royal Observatory at Greenwich, in London, was founded in 1675 by King Charles II to observe the moon and the stars.

The ancient Greeks believed that Earth was the center of the universe, and they listed the planets as the moon, the sun, Mercury, Venus, Mars, Jupiter, and Saturn. In 1543, Nicolaus Copernicus suggested a system in which Earth orbited the sun—an idea supported by Galileo. The Catholic Church, however, insisted that Earth was the center of the universe and accused Galileo of heresy. In 1632, Galileo was forced to withdraw his support for the theory and was imprisoned in his home until he died in 1642.

Cannonball in Space

Following the logic of the universal law of gravitation, Newton imagined what would happen if a cannonball were fired from a high point above Earth. If the cannonball traveled too slowly, gravity would pull it back to Earth. If it were fired with too much force, it would escape from Earth's gravity and fly off into space. However, he figured out that with the right force to give the right speed, the cannonball would orbit Earth—a brilliant and accurate thought experiment.

SUPERHERO FACT

Wow!

Eight planets orbit the sun, though only six were known to Newton. Newton's work did much to explain the movements of those planets.

Yet, within a few decades, by the time Newton and other members of the Royal Society were discussing their ideas, it was generally accepted that the sun was at the center of a group of planets, although Neptune and Uranus were still undiscovered. What now interested astronomers was the path that the planets took in orbiting the sun—was it a circle or an oval-shaped ellipse, or something more like that of a comet?

John Flamsteed, the first Astronomer Royal, used a telescope in the newly built Royal Observatory in Greenwich, London, to observe and record how the stars moved across the sky. These records helped Newton with his work on the planets and the moon.

HALLEY STEPS IN

An illustration from 1770 shows the transit, or movement, of Venus across the sun. Newton's theories on how planets orbited the sun allowed later astronomers to make new discoveries.

Edmond Halley was a great admirer of Newton's work. He had discussed the movement of planets with Robert Hooke and Christopher Wren, but mistrusted Hooke's insistence that planets must follow a circular path around the sun. In 1684, Halley decided to visit Newton in Cambridge to find out what he thought.

When Halley asked what orbit a body would follow, he was amazed when Newton replied immediately that the path was an ellipse. Newton knew this partly from his studies of earlier scientists, such as Kepler, but mostly because he had already done the math that proved this was the case.

STAR CONTRIBUTION

Science Beats Superstition

Since ancient times, people had believed that the appearance and movement of planets and stars in the night sky influenced their lives, bringing good or bad luck. Many associated the plague in England, for instance, with the comet of 1664 and 1665. However, by the end of the seventeenth century, science had turned its back on such superstitions. Newton played a key role in this, showing that planetary motion was not magic but governed by sound mathematical principles.

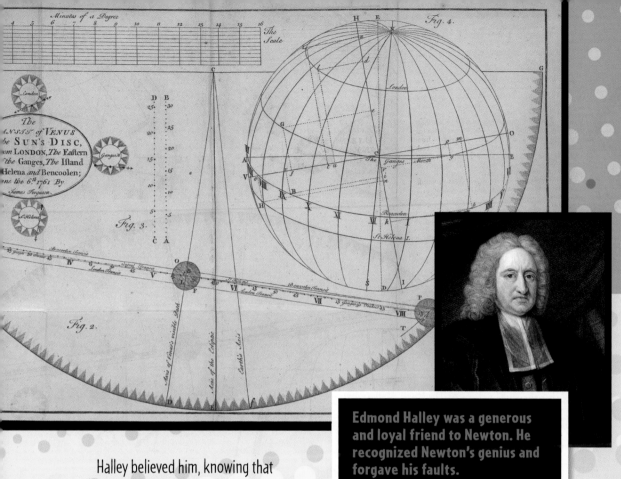

Fig. 4.

The Scale

Minutes of a Degree

The ANSIT of VENUS the SUN's DISC, from LONDON, The Eastern the Ganges, The Island Helena and Bencoolen; ane the 6.ᵗʰ 1761 By James Ferguson.

Fig. 3.

Fig. 2.

Halley believed him, knowing that Newton was probably the only mathematician of his time who could make such calculations, and he urged Newton to publish his work. However, Newton then found that he had lost his original figures. He promised to figure them all out again and send them to Halley.

True to his word, Newton rewrote his calculations and theory of gravitation in his paper *De Motu Corporum in Gyrum* ("About the Motion of Orbiting Bodies"), which he sent to Halley in November 1684, and which Halley then reported to the Royal Society. However, this time Newton's work upset John Flamsteed, who thought that Newton should have acknowledged that much of the paper was based on his own observations. Newton hit back by claiming that Flamsteed had slowed him down by taking so long to pass on his recorded observations! This is another example of Newton's sensitivity and hot temper bringing him into conflict with his colleagues. Had Newton been more tactful, he could have avoided arguments that upset him deeply.

NEWTON'S MASTERPIECE

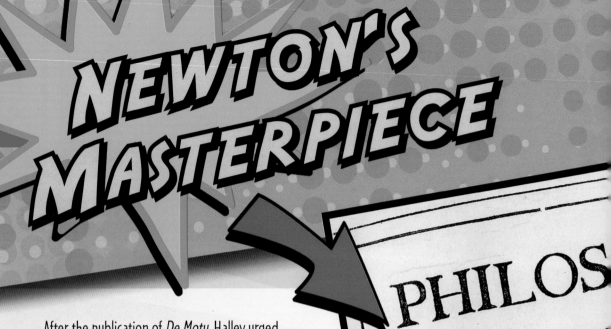

After the publication of *De Motu*, Halley urged Newton to publish all his work on the three laws of motion, together with his research on the law of gravitation. Newton agreed because he was becoming worried that someone else might publish ideas similar to his own.

The work was published in 1687 in three volumes and was named *Philosophiae Naturalis Principia Mathematica* –often shortened to the *Principia*, meaning "Principles." The first volume covered motion, the second discussed resistance, and the third explored the consequences of gravitation.

Although Newton had already figured out his laws of motion in the 1660s, it took him two years to write the *Principia*, avoiding most other work to get it done. The finished work shows how fully he had developed his ideas since his early work in Woolsthorpe. Newton showed that physical forces act according to rules and his equations give the mathematical basis for them.

PHILOS

NATU

PRIN

MATHE

Autore JS. NEWTON
Professore Lucasia

IMP

S. PEPY

World-changing Work

The *Principia* is probably the most important book about science ever published. It gave people the precise laws and equations needed to calculate force, mass, and acceleration in different situations, including the gravitational force between two objects in space. The *Principia* made Newton a scientific superstar in his day and ever since.

STAR CONTRIBUTION

The work would not have been published without Halley's help. He not only encouraged Newton in his writing but also found and liaised with the printer. He read and corrected the proofs and even paid for the printing with his own money. In a letter to Newton, written on July 5, 1687, Halley says, "I have at length brought your Book to an end, and hope it will please you. The last errata [corrections] came just in time to be inserted."

Robert Hooke, however, was far from pleased with the *Principia*. He thought that his correspondence with Newton had made a contribution that should have been acknowledged. Newton reacted with typical anger. He was so furious with Hooke that he deleted every single mention of him from the third volume of the work.

OPHIÆ
ALIS
CIPIA
MATICA.

Trin. Coll. Cantab. Soc. Matheseos & Societatis Regalis Sodali.

IMATU
Reg. Soc. PRA
Julii 5. 1686;

Kpow!

The title page of the first edition of Newton's *Principia* includes the word "Imprimatur," which means "let it be printed." It shows that the famous diarist Samuel Pepys gave the go-ahead for the printing.

FAME AND MADNESS

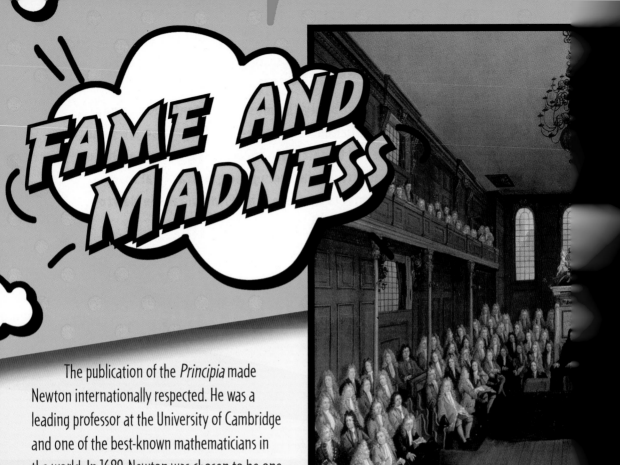

The publication of the *Principia* made Newton internationally respected. He was a leading professor at the University of Cambridge and one of the best-known mathematicians in the world. In 1689, Newton was chosen to be one of two Members of Parliament elected by the university, a role at the heart of English government, based in London. His success and acclaim, however, did not bring him happiness.

Newton's quarrel with Robert Hooke did not help. His dislike of Hooke was so great that Newton withdrew from the Royal Society and did not return until Hooke was no longer there, ten years later. Newton's state of mind worsened in 1693, when he suffered what today would be termed a nervous breakdown, but which Newton himself named "distemper" and "melancholia," attributed partly to bad digestion and a lack of sleep.

In Isaac Newton's day, Members of Parliament met in St. Stephen's Chapel in Westminster. The chapel was later destroyed by fire in 1834.

All-purpose Remedy

Newton was often bad tempered and anxious about his health. He stayed in bed when he had a cold and often mixed up his own medicine—a remedy named Leucatello's Balsam. It contained turpentine, rose water, beeswax, and olive oil, among other ingredients. Newton drank this to combat colds, measles, plague, smallpox, and other conditions. He also applied it directly to dog bites and bruises. Questionable though the mixture sounds, it clearly did not affect his health long term. At a time when the average life span was around 40 years, Newton survived until he was 84!

SUPERHERO FACT

Newton's friends became concerned that he was going mad, particularly when he wrote two strange letters—one to the renowned English diarist Samuel Pepys and the other to the philosopher John Locke —in which he told them he did not want to continue his acquaintance with them. Newton later apologized for the letters and said that he had not slept well for two weeks and not a wink for five nights!

Historians have suggested various possible causes of Newton's breakdown. In 1689, Newton had formed a close friendship with a Swiss mathematician named Nicholas Fatio de Duillier. He was probably the closest friend that Newton ever had, and he was devastated when the friendship ended in 1693. Another theory is that Newton was suffering from temporary madness caused by mercury or other substances, taken during his experiments with alchemy.

Samuel Pepys was a member of the Royal Society and knew Newton well. He is now best known for his diaries of London life in the 1660s.

Chapter 6

RECOGNITION AND REWARDS

After the publication of the *Principia*, Newton spent much less time on scientific work. When his state of mind and health recovered, he turned his attention to other things and took a much more active role in public life. He began to enjoy his celebrity and mixed with famous people of the time. He even dined with King William III.

In 1696, a friend of Newton's at Trinity College, who later became the Earl of Halifax, helped Newton to get the job of Warden at the Royal Mint. The Royal Mint was the building in London where coins were manufactured.

SUPERHERO FACT

Respect at Last

In his later years, Newton finally received the recognition and honors his great achievements merited. Three years after his appointment as Warden of the Mint, he was made Master of the Mint. In 1701, he was reelected Member of Parliament for the University of Cambridge and, in 1703, finally became President of the Royal Society. In 1705, a year after his work *Opticks* was published to great acclaim, he was knighted by King William and became Sir Isaac Newton.

When Newton was Warden of the Royal Mint, it was housed in the Tower of London. In 1811, it moved to this building in the City of London.

Newton left Cambridge and moved to London, where he threw himself into his new post. The job was well paid by the government and made Newton a rich man.

Newton was not expected to work hard at the Royal Mint, but he took the job seriously and introduced important improvements. At that time, forging coins was common, either by clipping bits of valuable metal off them or by producing fake coins. Newton used his knowledge of alchemy to design new coins, which were harder to forge. He also worked hard to catch and prosecute forgers.

In March 1703, Newton's old enemy Robert Hooke died, and this freed Newton to become active in the Royal Society again. Before the year was out, he was elected President of the Society and the following year he published *Opticks*, an account of his work on color and light. Hooke could not criticize it now!

William and his wife, Mary, arrived in London from Holland in 1689 and were confirmed as joint king and queen by the parliaments of Scotland and England.

RAGE AND REVENGE

Science superheroes are geniuses but not necessarily angels! Newton continued to quarrel and fly into rages. Worse still, he used his position as President of the Royal Society to get his own way. In particular, Newton abused his power to prevent Gottfried Leibniz, a prominent German mathematician, from receiving the acknowledgment that his contribution to the invention of calculus deserved.

> Gottfried Leibniz was a German mathematician who had visited the Royal Society in 1673, where he demonstrated his invention of a calculating machine.

Newton's quarrels with Leibniz had begun in 1684, when Leibniz published papers on calculus, 20 years after Newton's own work on the subject. The problem was that Newton did not publish his work on calculus until 1704, as part of his book *Opticks*, and so it seemed as though Newton had got his ideas from Leibniz. However, that suggestion made Newton furious, and each man accused the other of stealing. As President of the Royal Society, Newton set up an "impartial" committee to decide the issue, but in fact he wrote the report himself! It is now known that both men had come to the same conclusions independently of each other.

Light Fantastic

Newton waited until Robert Hooke had died before he published his book *Opticks*. It presented his previous work on light and color in a new way. Instead of putting forward his ideas as a theory, he proved them by reason and by experiments. It also included his work on calculus. *Opticks* was easier to understand than his previous papers on the subject, and the book became a model for how experiments in physics should be presented.

STAR CONTRIBUTION

In his final years, Newton had problems with his kidneys and lungs, and was looked after by his niece Catherine and her husband. A few weeks before he died, he burned his personal papers, which means that much about his life remains a mystery. He died on March 20, 1727, and was buried in Westminster Abbey, in London, among kings, queens, and other famous people.

Newton's work is still celebrated and explored. Historians study his notebooks and seek to decode them. A new translation of a page of his notes on alchemy was published in 2005. His original notebooks and books are held in libraries and universities, including Trinity College in Cambridge and St. Andrews in Scotland.

Blam!

Both Newton and Leibniz are now credited with developing calculus. In particular, Leibniz's mathematical symbols are still used today.

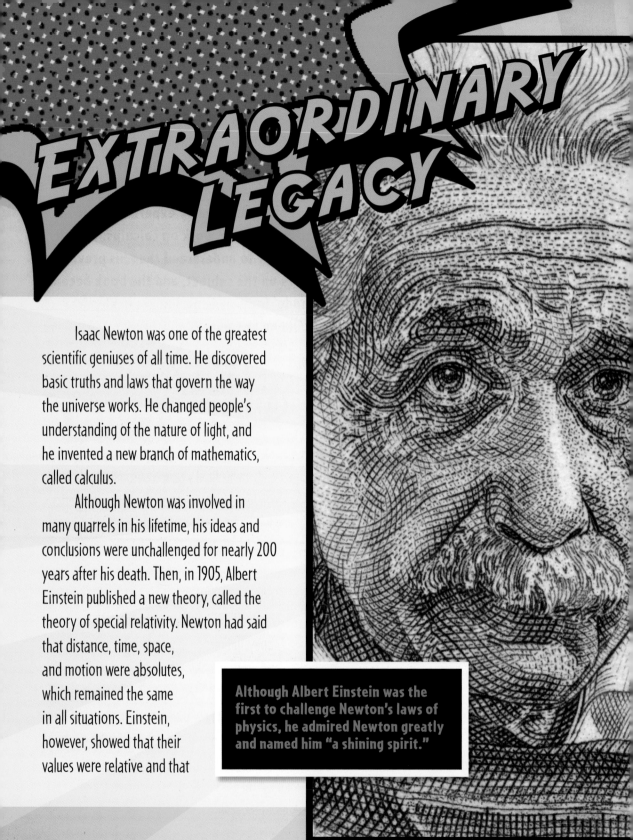

EXTRAORDINARY LEGACY

Isaac Newton was one of the greatest scientific geniuses of all time. He discovered basic truths and laws that govern the way the universe works. He changed people's understanding of the nature of light, and he invented a new branch of mathematics, called calculus.

Although Newton was involved in many quarrels in his lifetime, his ideas and conclusions were unchallenged for nearly 200 years after his death. Then, in 1905, Albert Einstein published a new theory, called the theory of special relativity. Newton had said that distance, time, space, and motion were absolutes, which remained the same in all situations. Einstein, however, showed that their values were relative and that

Although Albert Einstein was the first to challenge Newton's laws of physics, he admired Newton greatly and named him "a shining spirit."

What We Owe to Newton

While modern science has overtaken some of Newton's amazing achievements more than 300 years ago, many are still of great value. He was one of the pioneers of scientific method. His reflecting telescope surpassed all others of his age. He was the first to recognize that white light contains all the colors of the spectrum. His three laws of motion and law of universal gravity also remain broadly valid except in extreme situations or when total precision is required.

STAR CONTRIBUTION

Newton's laws did not hold in extreme circumstances, such as when something travels extremely fast–close to the speed of light–or if masses are very large.

There is still much to learn about our world and universe. One of Robert Hooke's criticisms of the *Principia* was that the book did not explain what causes gravity. Why do objects attract each other? Scientists still cannot answer this question. One current idea is that the "graviton," a special particle in each atom, exerts the force of gravity. Although some of the world's best scientific minds are searching for them, the particles have not yet been discovered.

Newton found simple laws that apply throughout the universe. Now scientists want to find a "theory of everything" to apply to even the smallest particles inside atoms. Newton would have been fascinated!

This powerful statue of Isaac Newton is by sculptor Eduardo Paolozzi. It shows Newton measuring with a compass.

Glossary

acceleration in physics, acceleration is the rate of change of speed or velocity

alchemy the attempt to change one metal into another using magic and other unscientific methods

apothecary a person who mixed up medicines and remedies–the equivalent of a pharmacist today

astronomy the scientific study of outer space, including planets, moons, and stars

atoms the tiniest parts of "elements," which are single, basic substances, such as hydrogen, copper, or gold

bachelor's degree the first degree that a student takes at university

bubonic plague a highly infectious disease, which can spread quickly, and which, in the past, killed from 30 percent to 90 percent of people in areas were it struck

calculus a branch of advanced mathematics that deals with quantities that are constantly changing

comets objects in space, made of dust and ice, which travel around the sun, and develop a long, bright tail–visible from Earth–when they are so close to the sun that some of the ice melts

diarist a person who records their thoughts, ideas, and experiences every day in a diary

Enlightenment intellectual movement in Europe in the seventeenth and eighteenth centuries, which celebrated the use of reason to figure out new ideas about God, nature, and human life

equation in mathematics, a formula that states that one expression (usually in numbers or letters) is equal to another

eyepiece the part of a telescope you look through

force a push or a pull that makes an object start to move or change the speed or direction it is moving in

galaxies vast groups of billions of stars that move together through space

gravity the force of attraction between two objects–in particular the force that pulls all objects toward the center of Earth

inertia the tendency of matter to resist change, remaining still or moving at a steady speed in a straight line, until it is affected by another active force

mass the amount of matter that an object contains

master's degree a more advanced degree taken after a bachelor's degree

matter anything–solids, liquids, and air–that has mass and takes up space

momentum a force produced by a moving body, which increases with speed and mass

orbits moves in a fixed path around another object

photons particles of light

prism a transparent object, usually made of glass or plastic, that refracts light to form the different colors of the spectrum

react act in response to something such as a force

refracts bends or changes direction. A beam of light refracts when it passes from one material to another

satellite a natural object (such as a moon) or manmade spacecraft that orbits a larger planet in space

scientific method the official name for all the techniques that scientists use to test new knowledge, including observation, measurable evidence, and clear procedures for testing and analyzing data, so that other scientists can confirm the findings

spectrum the range of visible colors, which each merge into the next

stationary not moving

thought experiment an experiment conducted by thinking through a situation, rather than trying it out

tutor a teacher at a university or college, who is responsible for the studies of a particular student or group of students

velocity the speed and direction in which an object is moving

For More Information

Books

Fandel, Jennifer. *Louis Pasteur and Pasteurization* (Graphic Library). Mankato, MN: Capstone, 2007.

Hollihan, Kerrie Logan. *Isaac Newton and Physics for Kids*. Chicago, IL: Chicago Review Press, 2009.

Lynette, Rachel. *Gravity: Forces and Motion* (Do It Yourself). North Mankato, MN: Heinemann-Raintree, 2009.

Steele, Philip. *Isaac Newton: The Scientist Who Changed Everything*. Washington, DC: National Geographic Society, 2013.

Websites

For a short biography of Newton and his laws of motion explained with animated graphics, see:
http://teachertech.rice.edu/Participants/louviere/Newton/law1.html

To read about Newton's life and the lives of other famous scientists, go to:
www.famousscientists.org/isaac-newton

Look here for more information on Newton's laws of motion and an illustrative NASA-eClips video:
www.physics4kids.com/files/motion_laws.html

See NASA's website for children for an animated diagram showing how Einstein's idea of gravity works in space:
http://spaceplace.nasa.gov/what-is-gravity

Index